CAROLS FOR CHOIRS

WORDS BOOKLET

Edited and arranged by
David Willcocks and John Rutter

Illustrations by
Christine Emery

T his booklet contains the words of fifty well-known carols and hymns which can be sung by congregation or audience. Most of these are for Christmas, with the addition of some Advent, Epiphany, and Easter items. Virtually all appear in *100 Carols for Choirs* or earlier *Carols for Choirs* volumes, though in some cases the choral arrangements in those books are not intended for congregational or audience participation.

The texts accord with those in most hymnals and in the *Carols for Choirs* series*, though punctuation, capitalization, and spelling have been standardized according to present-day usage.

* *See note at foot of next page*

Index of Titles and First Lines

Where first lines differ from titles, the former are shown in italic.
Numbers designate carol numbers.

Oxford University Press, Walton Street, Oxford
OX2 6DP, England
Oxford University Press, 200 Madison Avenue,
New York, NY 10016, USA

Oxford is a trade mark of Oxford University Press

© Oxford University Press 1987

POD

* Pre-1988 editions of *Carols for Choirs 1, 2,
3,* or *4* should be amended as follows:

  It came upon the midnight clear: V.4, line 7
should read 'give back the song'.

  Once in royal David's city: V.6, line 5
should read '*When* like stars'.

  While shepherds watched their flocks: V.6,
line 2 should read 'And *to* the earth'.

1 A great and mighty wonder

1 A great and mighty wonder,
  A full and holy cure!
The Virgin bears the Infant
  With virgin-honour pure.

    Repeat the hymn again!
      'To God on high be glory,
    And peace on earth to men!'

2 The Word becomes incarnate
  And yet remains on high!
And cherubim sing anthems
  To shepherds from the sky.

    Repeat the hymn again! (etc.)

3 While thus they sing your Monarch,
  Those bright angelic bands,
Rejoice, ye vales and mountains,
  Ye oceans, clap your hands.

    Repeat the hymn again! (etc.)

4 Since all he comes to ransom,
  By all be he adored,
The Infant born in Bethl'em,
  The Saviour and the Lord.

    Repeat the hymn again! (etc.)

5 And idol forms shall perish,
  And error shall decay,
And Christ shall wield his sceptre,
  Our Lord and God for ay.

    Repeat the hymn again! (etc.)

St Germanus (634–734)
tr. J. M. Neale (1818–66)

2 All my heart this night rejoices

1 All my heart this night rejoices
    As I hear,
    Far and near,
Sweetest angel voices:
'Christ is born!' their choirs are singing,
    Till the air
    Ev'rywhere
Now with joy is ringing.

2 Hark! a voice from yonder manger,
    Soft and sweet,
    Doth entreat,
'Flee from woe and danger!
Brethren, come! from all doth grieve you,
    You are freed;
    All you need
I will surely give you.'

3 Come, then, let us hasten yonder!
    Here let all,
    Great and small,
Kneel in awe and wonder!
Love him who with love is yearning!
    Hail the star
    That from far
Bright with hope is burning!

4 Thee, dear Lord, with heed I'll cherish,
    Live to thee,
    And with thee,
Dying, shall not perish;
But shall dwell with thee for ever,
    Far on high,
    In the joy
That can alter never.

Paul Gerhardt (1607–76)
tr. Catherine Winkworth (1827–78)

3 *Angels, from the realms of glory*

1 Angels, from the realms of glory,
   Wing your flight o'er all the earth;
Ye who sang creation's story,
   Now proclaim Messiah's birth:

   Come and worship
     Christ, the new-born King;
   Come and worship,
     Worship Christ, the new-born King.

2 Shepherds, in the field abiding,
   Watching o'er your flocks by night,
God with man is now residing,
   Yonder shines the Infant Light:

   Come and worship, (etc.)

3 Sages, leave your contemplations,
   Brighter visions beam afar;
Seek the great Desire of Nations,
   Ye have seen his natal star:

   Come and worship, (etc.)

4 Saints before the altar bending,
   Watching long in hope and fear,
Suddenly the Lord, descending,
   In his temple shall appear:

   Come and worship, (etc.)

5 Though an infant now we view him,
   He shall fill his Father's throne,
Gather all the nations to him;
   Every knee shall then bow down:

   Come and worship, (etc.)

6 All creation, join in praising
   God the Father, Spirit, Son,
Evermore your voices raising
   To th'eternal Three in One:

   Come and worship, (etc.)

James Montgomery (1771–1854)

4 *Angels, from the realms of glory*

1 Angels, from the realms of glory,
   Wing your flight o'er all the earth;
Ye who sang creation's story,
   Now proclaim Messiah's birth:

   Gloria in excelsis Deo,
   Gloria in excelsis Deo!

2 Shepherds, in the field abiding,
   Watching o'er your flocks by night,
God with man is now residing,
   Yonder shines the Infant Light:

   Gloria in excelsis Deo, (etc.)

3 Sages, leave your contemplations,
   Brighter visions beam afar;
Seek the great Desire of Nations,
   Ye have seen his natal star:

   Gloria in excelsis Deo, (etc.)

4 Saints before the altar bending,
   Watching long in hope and fear,
Suddenly the Lord, descending,
   In his temple shall appear:

   Gloria in excelsis Deo, (etc.)

5 Though an infant now we view him,
   He shall fill his Father's throne,
Gather all the nations to him;
   Every knee shall then bow down:

   Gloria in excelsis Deo, (etc.)

James Montgomery (1771–1854)
Refrain altered

5 As with gladness men of old

1   As with gladness men of old
    Did the guiding star behold,
    As with joy they hailed its light,
    Leading onward, beaming bright,
    So, most gracious God, may we
    Evermore be led to thee.

2   As with joyful steps they sped
    To that lowly manger-bed,
    There to bend the knee before
    Him whom heaven and earth adore,
    So may we with willing feet
    Ever seek thy mercy-seat.

3   As they offered gifts most rare
    At that manger rude and bare,
    So may we with holy joy,
    Pure, and free from sin's alloy,
    All our costliest treasures bring,
    Christ, to thee our heavenly King.

4   Holy Jesu, every day
    Keep us in the narrow way;
    And, when earthly things are past,
    Bring our ransomed souls at last
    Where they need no star to guide,
    Where no clouds thy glory hide.

5   In the heav'nly country bright
    Need they no created light;
    Thou its Light, its Joy, its Crown,
    Thou its Sun which goes not down:
    There for ever may we sing
    Alleluyas to our King.

William Chatterton Dix (1837–98)

6 Birthday carol

(All) 1   Rejoice today with one accord,
              Alleluia!
          This is the birthday of our Lord.
              Alleluia!

              Gloria, gloria in excelsis,
                Gloria, gloria Deo!
              Gloria, gloria in excelsis,
                Gloria, gloria Deo!

(Women) 2 Shepherds abiding in the field,
              Alleluia!
          To them God's glory was reveal'd.
              Alleluia!

              Gloria, gloria in excelsis, (etc.)

(Men) 3   And to the shepherds sore afraid
              Alleluia!
          An angel said, 'Be not dismayed,'
              Alleluia!

              Gloria, gloria in excelsis, (etc.)

(Women) 4 'Tidings of joy to you I bring,'
              Alleluia!
          'Today is born a heav'nly King.'
              Alleluia!

              Gloria, gloria in excelsis, (etc.)

(Men) 5   'And ye shall find in manger laid,'
              Alleluia!
          'The Babe in swaddling clothes arrayed.'
              Alleluia!

              Gloria, gloria in excelsis, (etc.)

(Women) 6 A host of angels filled the sky
              Alleluia!
          Thus singing praise to God on high:
              Alleluia!

              Gloria, gloria in excelsis, (etc.)

(All) 7   Now join we all the angel-throng,
              Alleluia!
          And let our voices swell the song:
              Alleluia!

              Gloria, gloria in excelsis,
                Gloria, gloria Deo!
              Gloria, gloria in excelsis,
                Gloria, gloria Deo!

David Willcocks (b.1919)

*Audience/congregation may join in these lines.

7 Away in a manger

1 Away in a manger, no crib for a bed,
The little Lord Jesus laid down his sweet head;
The stars in the bright sky looked down where he lay
The little Lord Jesus asleep on the hay.

2 The cattle are lowing, the baby awakes,
But little Lord Jesus no crying he makes.
I love thee, Lord Jesus! Look down from the sky,
And stay by my side until morning is nigh.

3 Be near me, Lord Jesus; I ask thee to stay
Close by me for ever, and love me, I pray.
Bless all the dear children in thy tender care,
And fit us for heaven, to live with thee there.

Anon. American, published 1885

8 Child in a manger

1 Child in a manger, Jesus our Saviour,
  Born of a virgin holy and mild;
Sent from the highest, come down in glory;
  Tell the glad story, welcome the child.

2 Shepherds, arise now, go to the manger;
  Find where the infant Jesus is laid.
Offer your homage, kneel down before him;
  Praise and adore him, be not afraid.

3 Wise men, come seek him—Christ our Redeemer;
  Journey to Bethlem, led by a star.
Offer your treasures: gold, myrrh, and incense,
  Precious oblations brought from afar.

4 Praise to the Christ-child; praise to his mother;
  Glory to God our Father above.
Angels are singing songs of rejoicing,
  Greeting the infant born of God's love.

John Rutter (b. 1945)
based on a Gaelic carol

9 Ding dong! merrily on high

1 Ding dong! merrily on high
  In heav'n the bells are ringing:
Ding dong! verily the sky
  Is riv'n with angel-singing.

  Gloria! Hosanna in excelsis!

2 E'en so here below, below,
  Let steeple bells be swungen,
And *i-o, i-o, i-o,*
  By priest and people sungen.

  Gloria! Hosanna in excelsis!

3 Pray you, dutifully prime
  Your matin chime, ye ringers;
May you beautifully rime
  Your evetime song, ye singers.

  Gloria! Hosanna in excelsis!

G. R. Woodward (1848–1934)

i-o pronounced *ee-o*

10 God rest you merry, gentlemen

1 God rest you merry, gentlemen,
　Let nothing you dismay,
For Jesus Christ our Saviour
　Was born upon this day,
To save us all from Satan's power
　When we were gone astray:

　　O tidings of comfort and joy,
　　Comfort and joy,
　　O tidings of comfort and joy.

2 From God our heav'nly Father
　A blessèd angel came,
And unto certain shepherds
　Brought tidings of the same,
How that in Bethlehem was born
　The Son of God by name:

　　O tidings of comfort and joy, (etc.)

3 The shepherds at those tidings
　Rejoicèd much in mind,
And left their flocks a-feeding,
　In tempest, storm and wind,
And went to Bethlehem straightway
　This blessèd babe to find:

　　O tidings of comfort and joy, (etc.)

4 But when to Bethlehem they came,
　Whereat this infant lay,
They found him in a manger,
　Where oxen feed on hay;
His mother Mary kneeling,
　Unto the Lord did pray:

　　O tidings of comfort and joy, (etc.)

5 Now to the Lord sing praises,
　All you within this place,
And with true love and brotherhood
　Each other now embrace;
This holy tide of Christmas
　All others doth deface*:

　　O tidings of comfort and joy, (etc.)

English traditional carol

*deface=outshine

11 Gabriel's message

1 The angel Gabriel from heaven came,
His wings as drifted snow, his eyes as flame;
'All hail,' said he, 'thou lowly maiden Mary,

　　Most highly favour'd lady,'
　　Gloria!

2 'For known a blessed Mother thou shalt be,
All generations laud and honour thee,
Thy Son shall be Emmanuel, by seers foretold,

　　Most highly favour'd lady,'
　　Gloria!

3 Then gentle Mary meekly bowed her head,
'To me be as it pleaseth God,' she said,
'My soul shall laud and magnify his holy name.'

　　Most highly favour'd lady,
　　Gloria!

4 Of her, Emmanuel, the Christ, was born
In Bethlehem, all on a Christmas morn,
And Christian folk throughout the world will
　ever say:
　　Most highly favour'd lady,
　　Gloria!

Sabine Baring-Gould (1834–1924)

13 Good King Wenceslas

(All) 1 Good King Wenceslas looked out,
On the Feast of Stephen,
When the snow lay round about,
Deep, and crisp, and even:
Brightly shone the moon that night,
Though the frost was cruel,
When a poor man came in sight,
Gath'ring winter fuel.

(Men) 2 'Hither, page, and stand by me,
If thou know'st it, telling,
Yonder peasant, who is he?
Where and what his dwelling?'
(Women) 'Sire, he lives a good league hence,
Underneath the mountain,
Right against the forest fence,
By Saint Agnes' fountain.'

(Men) 3 'Bring me flesh, and bring me wine,
Bring me pine-logs hither:
Thou and I will see him dine,
When we bear them thither.'
(All) Page and monarch, forth they went,
Forth they went together;
Through the rude wind's wild lament
And the bitter weather.

12 Good Christian men, rejoice

1 Good Christian men, rejoice
With heart and soul and voice;
Give ye heed to what we say,
Jesus Christ is born today:
Ox and ass before him bow,
And he is in the manger now.
Christ is born today,
Christ is born today!

2 Good Christian men, rejoice
With heart and soul and voice;
Now ye hear of endless bliss,
Jesus Christ was born for this:
He hath opened heaven's door,
And man is blest for evermore.
Christ was born for this,
Christ was born for this!

3 Good Christian men, rejoice
With heart and soul and voice;
Now ye need not fear the grave,
Jesus Christ was born to save,
Calls you one and calls you all,
To gain his everlasting hall.
Christ was born to save,
Christ was born to save!

J. M. Neale (1818–66), *altered*

(Women) 4 'Sire, the night is darker now,
And the wind blows stronger;
Fails my heart, I know not how;
I can go no longer.'
(Men) 'Mark my footsteps, good my page;
Tread thou in them boldly:
Thou shalt find the winter's rage
Freeze thy blood less coldly.'

(All) 5 In his master's steps he trod,
Where the snow lay dinted;
Heat was in the very sod
Which the saint had printed.
Therefore, Christian men, be sure,
Wealth or rank possessing,
Ye who now will bless the poor,
Shall yourselves find blessing.

J. M. Neale (1818–66)

14 Here we come a-wassailing

1 Here we come a-wassailing
  Among the leaves so green,
Here we come a-wandering,
  So fair to be seen:

  Love and joy come to you,
  And to you, your wassail too,
  And God bless you, and send you
    A happy New Year,
  And God send you a happy New Year.

2 Our wassail cup is made
  Of the rosemary tree,
And so is your beer
  Of the best barley:

  Love and joy come to you, (etc.)

3 We are not daily beggars
  That beg from door to door,
But we are neighbours' children
  Whom you have seen before:

  Love and joy come to you, (etc.)

4 Call up the butler of this house,
  Put on his golden ring;
Let him bring us up a glass of beer,
  And better we shall sing:

  Love and joy come to you, (etc.)

5 We have got a little purse
  Of stretching leather skin;
We want a little of your money
  To line it well within:

  Love and joy come to you, (etc.)

6 Bring us out a table,
  And spread it with a cloth;
Bring us out a mouldy cheese,
  And some of your Christmas loaf:

  Love and joy come to you, (etc.)

7 God bless the master of this house,
  Likewise the mistress too;
And all the little children
  That round the table go:

  Love and joy come to you, (etc.)

8 Good master and good mistress,
  While you're sitting by the fire,
Pray think of us poor children
  Who are wand'ring in the mire:

  Love and joy come to you, (etc.)

English traditional carol

15 Hark! the herald-angels sing

1 Hark! the herald-angels sing
  Glory to the new-born King;
Peace on earth and mercy mild,
God and sinners reconciled:
Joyful all ye nations rise,
Join the triumph of the skies;
With th'angelic host proclaim,
Christ is born in Bethlehem.
  Hark! the herald-angels sing
  Glory to the new-born King.

2 Christ, by highest heav'n adored,
Christ, the everlasting Lord,
Late in time behold him come,
Offspring of a virgin's womb!
Veiled in flesh the Godhead see,
Hail th'incarnate Deity,
Pleased as Man with man to dwell,
Jesus, our Emmanuel!
  Hark! the herald-angels sing
  Glory to the new-born King.

3 Hail the heav'n-born Prince of Peace!
Hail the Sun of Righteousness!
Light and life to all he brings,
Ris'n with healing in his wings;
Mild he lays his glory by,
Born that man no more may die,
Born to raise the sons of earth,
Born to give them second birth.
  Hark! the herald-angels sing
  Glory to the new-born King.

Charles Wesley (1707–88) and others

Deity pronounced Dee-ity

16 *In dulci jubilo*

1 *In dulci jubilo*
   Let us our homage shew;
   Our heart's joy reclineth
   In praesepio
   And like a bright star shineth
   Matris in gremio.
   Alpha es et O,
   Alpha es et O!

2 *O Jesu parvule*
   I yearn for thee alway!
   Hear me, I beseech thee,
   O Puer optime!
   My prayer let it reach thee,
   O Princeps gloriae!
   Trahe me post te,
   Trahe me post te!

3 *O Patris caritas,*
   O Nati lenitas!
   Deeply were we stainèd
   Per nostra crimina;
   But thou hast for us gainèd
   Coelorum gaudia.
   O that we were there,
   O that we were there!

4 *Ubi sunt gaudia,*
   If that they be not there?
   There are angels singing
   Nova cantica,
   And there the bells are ringing
   In Regis curia:
   O that we were there,
   O that we were there!

German, 14th cent.
tr. R. L. Pearsall (1795–1856)

17 *I saw three ships*

*(All children) 1 I saw three ships come sailing in,
         Come sailing in, come sailing in;
       I saw three ships come sailing in
         On Christmas Day in the morning.

(Boys) 2 Pray, whither sailed those ships all three,
       Those ships all three, those ships all three;
     Pray, whither sailed those ships all three
       On Christmas Day in the morning?

(Girls) 3 O, they sailed in to Bethlehem,
       To Bethlehem, to Bethlehem;
     O, they sailed in to Bethlehem
       On Christmas Day in the morning.

(All children) 4 And who should be in those three ships,
       In those three ships, in those three ships;
     And who should be in those three ships
       But Joseph and his Lady?

(Choir only) 5 And he did whistle and she did sing,
       And she did sing, and she did sing;
     And he did whistle and she did sing
       On Christmas Day in the morning.

6 *Boys whistle melody*

7 *Girls sing melody to 'la'*

(All children) 8 And all the bells on earth shall ring,
       On earth shall ring, on earth shall ring;
     And all the bells on earth shall ring
       On Christmas Day in the morning.

(Choir only) 9 And all the angels in heav'n shall sing,
       In heav'n shall sing, in heav'n shall sing;
     And all the angels in heav'n shall sing
       On Christmas Day in the morning.

(All children) 10 Then let us all rejoice amain,†
       Rejoice amain, rejoice amain;
     Then let us all rejoice amain
       On Christmas Day in the morning.

English traditional carol

*Bracketed instructions apply only to the arrangement by John Rutter in *Carols for Choirs 3* and *100 Carols for Choirs.*

†amain=greatly, immediately

18 *I saw three ships*

(Women) 1   I saw three ships come sailing in
      On Christmas Day, on Christmas Day,
    I saw three ships come sailing in
      On Christmas Day in the morning.

(Men) 2   And what was in those ships all three?

(Women) 3   Our Saviour Christ and his Lady.

(Men) 4   Pray, whither sailed those ships all three?

(Women) 5   O, they sailed into Bethlehem.

(Men) 6   And all the bells on earth shall ring.

(Women) 7   And all the angels in heav'n shall sing.

(Men) 8   And all the souls on earth shall sing.

(All) 9   Then let us all rejoice amain!*

English traditional carol

*amain=greatly, immediately

19 *Infant holy, infant lowly*

1 Infant holy, infant lowly,
   For his bed a cattle stall;
 Oxen lowing, little knowing
   Christ the Babe is Lord of all.
 Swift are winging angels singing,
 Nowells ringing, tidings bringing,
   Christ the Babe is Lord of all,
   Christ the Babe is Lord of all.

2 Flocks were sleeping, shepherds keeping
   Vigil till the morning new;
 Saw the glory, heard the story,
   Tidings of a gospel true.
 Thus rejoicing, free from sorrow,
 Praises voicing, greet the morrow,
   Christ the Babe was born for you,
   Christ the Babe was born for you!

Polish carol
tr. Edith M. Reed (1885–1933)

20 *It came upon the midnight clear*

1 It came upon the midnight clear,
   That glorious song of old,
 From angels bending near the earth
   To touch their harps of gold:
 'Peace on the earth, goodwill to men,
   From heaven's all-gracious King!'
 The world in solemn stillness lay
   To hear the angels sing.

2 Still through the cloven skies they come,
   With peaceful wings unfurled;
 And still their heav'nly music floats
   O'er all the weary world;
 Above its sad and lowly plains
   They bend on hov'ring wing;
 And ever o'er its Babel sounds
   The blessed angels sing.

3 Yet with the woes of sin and strife
   The world has suffered long;
 Beneath the angel-strain have rolled
   Two thousand years of wrong;
 And man, at war with man, hears not
   The love-song which they bring:
 O hush the noise, ye men of strife,
   And hear the angels sing!

4 For lo! the days are hastening on,
   By prophet-bards foretold,
 When, with the ever-circling years,
   Comes round the age of gold;
 When peace shall over all the earth
   Its ancient splendours fling,
 And the whole world give back the song
   Which now the angels sing.

E. H. Sears (1810–76)

21 *In the bleak mid-winter*

1 In the bleak mid-winter
    Frosty wind made moan,
Earth stood hard as iron,
    Water like a stone;
Snow had fallen, snow on snow,
    Snow on snow,
In the bleak mid-winter
    Long ago.

2 Our God, Heav'n cannot hold him
    Nor earth sustain;
Heav'n and earth shall flee away
    When he comes to reign:
In the bleak mid-winter
    A stable-place sufficed
The Lord God Almighty
    Jesus Christ.

3 Enough for him, whom cherubim
    Worship night and day,
A breastful of milk
    And a mangerful of hay;
Enough for him, whom angels
    Fall down before,
The ox and ass and camel
    Which adore.

4 Angels and archangels
    May have gathered there,
Cherubim and seraphim
    Thronged the air;
But only his mother
    In her maiden bliss
Worshipped the Beloved
    With a kiss.

5 What can I give him,
    Poor as I am?
If I were a shepherd
    I would bring a lamb,
If I were a Wise Man
    I would do my part,—
Yet what I can I give him,
    Give my heart.

Christina Rossetti (1830–94)

22 *Jingle, bells*

1 Dashing through the snow
    In a one-horse open sleigh,
O'er the fields we go,
    Laughing all the way;
Bells on Bobtail ring,
    Making spirits bright;
What fun it is to ride, and sing
    A sleighing song tonight!

  Jingle, bells, jingle, bells,
    Jingle all the way;
  Oh, what fun it is to ride
    In a one-horse open sleigh!
  Jingle, bells, jingle, bells,
    Jingle all the way;
  Oh, what fun it is to ride
    In a one-horse open sleigh!

2 Now the ground is white;
    Go it while you're young,
Take the girls tonight,
    And sing this sleighing song.
Just get a bob-tailed bay,
    Two-forty for his speed;
Then hitch him to an open sleigh
And crack! you'll take the lead.

  Jingle, bells, jingle, bells, (etc.)

James Pierpont (1822–93)

23 Jesus Christ is risen today

1 Jesus Christ is risen today, *Alleluya!*
   Our triumphant holy day, *Alleluya!*
   Who did once, upon the Cross, *Alleluya!*
   Suffer to redeem our loss. *Alleluya!*

2 Hymns of praise then let us sing, *Alleluya!*
   Unto Christ, our heav'nly King, *Alleluya!*
   Who endured the Cross and grave, *Alleluya!*
   Sinners to redeem and save. *Alleluya!*

3 But the pains that he endured, *Alleluya!*
   Our salvation have procured; *Alleluya!*
   Now above the sky he's King, *Alleluya!*
   Where the angels ever sing. *Alleluya!*

Lyra Davidica (1708)
and the *Supplement* (1816)

24 Joy to the world

1 Joy to the world! the Lord is come;
      Let earth receive her King.
   Let ev'ry heart prepare him room,
      And heav'n and nature sing,
         And heav'n and nature sing,
         And heav'n, and heav'n and nature sing.

2 Joy to the world! the Saviour reigns;
      Let men their songs employ,
   While fields and floods, rocks, hills and plains
      Repeat the sounding joy,
         Repeat the sounding joy,
         Repeat, repeat the sounding joy.

3 He rules the world with truth and grace,
      And makes the nations prove
   The glories of his righteousness
      And wonders of his love,
         And wonders of his love,
         And wonders, wonders of his love.

Isaac Watts (1674–1748)

25 Lo! he comes with clouds descending

1 Lo! he comes with clouds descending,
      Once for favoured sinners slain;
   Thousand thousand saints attending
      Swell the triumph of his train:
         Alleluya! (*3 times*)
      God appears, on earth to reign.

2 Every eye shall now behold him
      Robed in dreadful majesty;
   Those who set at nought and sold him,
      Pierced and nailed him to the tree,
         Deeply wailing (*3 times*)
      Shall the true Messiah see.

3 Those dear tokens of his passion
      Still his dazzling body bears,
   Cause of endless exultation
      To his ransomed worshippers:
         With what rapture (*3 times*)
      Gaze we on those glorious scars!

4 Yea, amen! let all adore thee,
      High on thine eternal throne;
   Saviour, take the power and glory:
      Claim the kingdom for thine own:
         O come quickly! (*3 times*)
      Alleluya! Come, Lord, come!

Charles Wesley (1707–88)
and John Cennick (1718–55)

26 Lord of the Dance

1 I danced in the morning
   When the world was begun,
And I danced in the moon
   And the stars and the sun;
And I came down from heaven
   And I danced on the earth,
At Bethlehem
   I had my birth.
   'Dance, then, wherever you may be,
   I am the Lord of the Dance,' said he,
   'And I'll lead you all, wherever you may be,
   And I'll lead you all in the Dance,' said he.

2 I danced for the scribe
   And the Pharisee,
But they would not dance
   And they wouldn't follow me.
I danced for the fishermen,
   For James and John—
They came with me
   And the Dance went on.
   'Dance, then, wherever you may be, (etc.)

3 I danced on the Sabbath
   And I cured the lame;
The holy people
   Said it was a shame.
They buried my body
   And they thought I'd gone—
But I am the Dance,
   And I still go on.
   'Dance, then, wherever you may be, (etc.)

4 I danced on a Friday
   When the sky turned black;
It's hard to dance
   With the devil on your back.
They whipped and they stripped
   And they hung me on high,
And they left me there
   On a cross to die.
   'Dance, then, wherever you may be, (etc.)

5 They cut me down
   And I leapt on high;
'I am the Life
   That'll never, never die.
I'll live in you
   If you'll live in me;
I am the Lord
   Of the Dance,' said he.
   'Dance, then, wherever you may be, (etc.)

In some hymnbooks lines 5–8 of   Sydney Carter (*b.* 1915)
verses 3 and 4 are transposed.

Reprinted by permission of Stainer and Bell Ltd., London, and Galaxy
Music Corporation, New York.

27 O little one sweet

1 O little one sweet, O little one mild,
   Thy Father's purpose thou hast fulfilled;
      Thou cam'st from heav'n to mortal ken,
      Equal to be with us poor men,
   O little one sweet, O little one mild.

2 O little one sweet, O little one mild,
   With joy thou hast the whole world filled;
      Thou camest here from heav'n's domain,
      To bring men comfort in their pain,
   O little one sweet, O little one mild.

3 O little one sweet, O little one mild,
   In thee love's beauties are all distilled;
      Then light in us thy love's bright flame,
      That we may give thee back the same,
   O little one sweet, O little one mild.

4 O little one sweet, O little one mild,
   Help us to do as thou hast willed.
      Lo, all we have belongs to thee!
      Ah, keep us in our fealty!
   O little one sweet, O little one mild.

Samuel Scheidt (1587–1654)
tr. Percy Dearmer (1867–1936)

28 O come, all ye faithful

1   O come, all ye faithful,
       Joyful and triumphant,
  O come ye, O come ye to Bethlehem;
       Come and behold him
       Born the King of Angels:

O come, let us adore him,
O come, let us adore him,
O come, let us adore him, Christ the Lord

2   God of God,
       Light of Light,
  Lo! he abhors not the Virgin's womb;
       Very God,
       Begotten, not created:

O come, let us adore him, (etc.)

3   See how the shepherds,
       Summoned to his cradle,
  Leaving their flocks, draw nigh with lowly fear;
       We too will thither
       Bend our joyful footsteps:

O come, let us adore him, (etc.)

4   Lo! star-led chieftains,
       Magi, Christ adoring,
  Offer him incense, gold, and myrrh;
       We to the Christ Child
       Bring our hearts' oblations:

O come, let us adore him, (etc.)

5   Child, for us sinners
       Poor and in the manger,
  Fain we embrace thee, with awe and love;
       Who would not love thee,
       Loving us so dearly?

O come, let us adore him, (etc.)

6   Sing, choirs of angels,
       Sing in exultation,
  Sing, all ye citizens of heaven above;
       Glory to God
       In the highest:

O come, let us adore him, (etc.)

7   Yea, Lord, we greet thee,
       Born this happy morning,
  Jesu, to thee be glory giv'n;
       Word of the Father,
       Now in flesh appearing:

O come, let us adore him, (etc.)

J. F Wade (c.1711–1786)
tr. Frederick Oakeley (1802–80) and others

29 O little town of Bethlehem

1   O little town of Bethlehem,
    How still we see thee lie!
  Above thy deep and dreamless sleep
    The silent stars go by.
  Yet in thy dark streets shineth
    The everlasting light;
  The hopes and fears of all the years
    Are met in thee tonight.

2   O morning stars, together
    Proclaim the holy birth,
  And praises sing to God the King,
    And peace to men on earth;
  For Christ is born of Mary;
    And, gathered all above,
  While mortals sleep, the angels keep
    Their watch of wondering love.

3   How silently, how silently,
    The wondrous gift is given!
  So God imparts to human hearts
    The blessings of his heav'n.
  No ear may hear his coming;
    But in this world of sin,
  Where meek souls will receive him, still
    The dear Christ enters in.

4   O holy Child of Bethlehem,
    Descend to us, we pray;
  Cast out our sin, and enter in,
    Be born in us today.
  We hear the Christmas angels
    The great glad tidings tell:
  O come to us, abide with us,
    Our Lord Emmanuel.

Phillips Brooks (1835–93)

30 *Of the Father's heart begotten*

1 Of the Father's heart begotten,
     Ere the world from chaos rose,
  He is Alpha: from that Fountain
     All that is and hath been flows;
  He is Omega, of all things
     Yet to come the mystic Close,
     Evermore and evermore.

2 By his word was all created;
     He commanded and 'twas done;
  Earth and sky and boundless ocean,
     Universe of three in one,
  All that sees the moon's soft radiance,
  All that breathes beneath the sun,
     Evermore and evermore.

3 He assumed this mortal body,
     Frail and feeble, doomed to die,
  That the race from dust created
     Might not perish utterly,
  Which the dreadful Law had sentenced
  In the depths of hell to lie,
     Evermore and evermore.

4 O how blest that wondrous birthday,
     When the Maid the curse retrieved,
  Brought to birth mankind's salvation,
     By the Holy Ghost conceived;
  And the Babe, the world's Redeemer,
     In her loving arms received,
     Evermore and evermore.

5 This is he, whom seer and sibyl
     Sang in ages long gone by;
  This is he of old revealèd
     In the page of prophecy;
  Lo! he comes, the promised Saviour;
     Let the world his praises cry!
     Evermore and evermore.

6 Sing, ye heights of heav'n, his praises;
     Angels and archangels, sing!
  Wheresoe'er ye be, ye faithful,
     Let your joyous anthems ring,
  Ev'ry tongue his name confessing,
  Countless voices answering,
     Evermore and evermore.

Prudentius (c.348–413)
tr. R. F. Davis (1866–1937)

Reprinted by permission of J. M. Dent & Sons Ltd.

31 *Once in royal David's city*

1 Once in royal David's city
     Stood a lowly cattle shed,
  Where a mother laid her baby
     In a manger for his bed:
  Mary was that mother mild,
  Jesus Christ her little child.

2 He came down to earth from heaven,
     Who is God and Lord of all,
  And his shelter was a stable,
     And his cradle was a stall;
  With the poor, and mean, and lowly,
  Lived on earth our Saviour holy.

3 And through all his wondrous childhood
     He would honour and obey,
  Love, and watch the lowly maiden,
     In whose gentle arms he lay;
  Christian children all must be
  Mild, obedient, good as he.

4 For he is our childhood's pattern,
     Day by day like us he grew,
  He was little, weak, and helpless,
     Tears and smiles like us he knew;
  And he feeleth for our sadness,
  And he shareth in our gladness.

5 And our eyes at last shall see him,
     Through his own redeeming love,
  For that child so dear and gentle
     Is our Lord in heav'n above;
  And he leads his children on
  To the place where he is gone.

6 Not in that poor lowly stable,
     With the oxen standing by,
  We shall see him; but in heaven,
     Set at God's right hand on high;
  When like stars his children crowned
  All in white shall wait around.

Cecil Frances Alexander (1818–95)

32 O come, O come, Emmanuel!

(All) 1 O come, O come, Emmanuel!
Redeem thy captive Israel,
That into exile drear is gone
Far from the face of God's dear Son.

Rejoice! Rejoice! Emmanuel
Shall come to thee, O Israel.

(Men) 2 O come, thou Branch of Jesse! draw
The quarry from the lion's claw;
From the dread caverns of the grave,
From nether hell, thy people save.

Rejoice! (etc.)

(Women) 3 O come, O come, thou Dayspring bright!
Pour on our souls thy healing light;
Dispel the long night's ling'ring gloom,
And pierce the shadows of the tomb.

Rejoice! (etc.)

(Men) 4 O come, thou Lord of David's Key!
The royal door fling wide and free;
Safeguard for us the heav'nward road,
And bar the way to death's abode.

Rejoice! (etc.)

(All) 5 O come, O come, Adonaï,
Who in thy glorious majesty
From that high mountain clothed with awe
Gavest thy folk the elder law.

Rejoice! (etc.)

18th cent.
tr. T. A. Lacey (1853–1931)

33 Personent hodie

1 Personent hodie
Voces puerulae,
Laudantes jucunde
   Qui nobis est natus,
   Summo Deo datus,
Et de vir-, vir-, vir-,
Et de vir-, vir-, vir-,
Et de virgineo
   Ventre procreatus.

2 In mundo nascitur,
Pannis involvitur,
Praesepi ponitur
   Stabulo brutorum,
   Rector supernorum.
Perdidit, -dit, -dit,
Perdidit, -dit, -dit,
Perdidit spolia
   Princeps infernorum.

3 Magi tres venerunt,
Parvulum inquirunt,
Bethlehem adeunt,*
   Stellulam sequendo,
   Ipsum adorando,
Aurum, thus, thus, thus,
Aurum, thus, thus, thus,
Aurum, thus, et myrrham
   Ei offerendo.

4 Omnes clericuli,
Pariter pueri,
Cantent ut angeli:
   Advenisti mundo,
   Laudes tibi fundo.
Ideo, -o, -o,
Ideo, -o, -o,
Ideo gloria
   In excelsis Deo!

from *Piae Cantiones* (1582)

* This line has been conjecturally
supplied. In the original, *Parvulum*
inquirunt was repeated.

34 Rocking

1 Little Jesus, sweetly sleep, do not stir;
We will lend a coat of fur,
    We will rock you, rock you, rock you,
    We will rock you, rock you, rock you:
See the fur to keep you warm,
Snugly round your tiny form.

2 Mary's little baby, sleep, sweetly sleep,
Sleep in comfort, slumber deep;
    We will rock you, rock you, rock you,
    We will rock you, rock you, rock you:
We will serve you all we can,
Darling, darling little man.

Czech traditional carol
tr. Percy Dearmer (1867–1936)

35 Sussex carol

1 On Christmas night all Christians sing,
To hear the news the angels bring,
On Christmas night all Christians sing,
To hear the news the angels bring—
    News of great joy, news of great mirth,
    News of our merciful King's birth.

2 Then why should men on earth be so sad,
Since our Redeemer made us glad,
Then why should men on earth be so sad,
Since our Redeemer made us glad?
    When from our sin he set us free,
    All for to gain our liberty?

3 When sin departs before his grace,
Then life and health come in its place,
When sin departs before his grace,
Then life and health come in its place;
    Angels and men with joy may sing,
    All for to see the new-born King.

4 All out of darkness we have light,
Which made the angels sing this night,
All out of darkness we have light,
Which made the angels sing this night:
    'Glory to God and peace to men,
    Now and for evermore. Amen.'

English traditional carol

36 See amid the winter's snow

(Women) 1 See amid the winter's snow,
Born for us on earth below;
See the tender Lamb appears,
Promised from eternal years.

(All)   *Hail, thou ever-blessed morn!*
    Hail, redemption's happy dawn!
    Sing through all Jerusalem,
    Christ is born in Bethlehem.

(All) 2 Lo, within a manger lies
He who built the starry skies;
He who, throned in height sublime,
Sits amid the cherubim:

(All)   *Hail, thou ever-blessed morn!* (etc.)

(Women) 3 Say, ye holy shepherds, say
What your joyful news today;
Wherefore have ye left your sheep
On the lonely mountain steep?

(All)   *Hail, thou ever-blessed morn!* (etc.)

(Men) 4 'As we watched at dead of night,
Lo, we saw a wondrous light;
Angels singing "Peace on earth"
Told us of the Saviour's birth.'

(All)   *Hail, thou ever-blessed morn!* (etc.)

(All) 5 Sacred Infant, all divine,
What a tender love was thine,
Thus to come from highest bliss
Down to such a world as this!

(All)   *Hail, thou ever-blessed morn!* (etc.)

(All) 6 Teach, O teach us, Holy Child,
By thy face so meek and mild,
Teach us to resemble thee,
In thy sweet humility:

(All)   *Hail, thou ever-blessed morn!* (etc.)

Edward Caswall (1814–78)

37 Sing aloud on this day!

1 Sing aloud on this day!
Children all raise the lay.
Cheerfully we and they
  Hasten to adore thee,
  Sent from highest glory,
For us born, born, born,
For us born, born, born,
For us born on this morn
  Of the Virgin Mary.

2 Now a child he is born,
Swathing bands him adorn,
Manger bed he'll not scorn,
  Ox and ass are near him;
  We as Lord revere him,
And the vain, vain, vain,
And the vain, vain, vain,
And the vain powers of hell
  Spoiled of prey now fear him.

3 From the far Orient
Guiding star wise men sent;
Him to seek their intent,
  Lord of all creation;
  Kneel in adoration.
Gifts of gold, gold, gold,
Gifts of gold, gold, gold,
Gifts of gold, frankincense,
  Myrrh for their oblation.

4 All must join him to praise;
Men and boys voices raise
On this day of all days;
  Angel voices ringing,
  Christmas tidings bringing.
Join we all, all, all,
Join we all, all, all,
Join we all, 'Gloria
  In excelsis' singing.

from *Piae Cantiones* (1582)
tr. John A. Parkinson (*b.* 1920)

38 Star carol

(Choir) 1 Sing this night, for a boy is born in Bethlehem,
Christ our Lord in a lowly manger lies;
Bring your gifts, come and worship at his cradle,
  Hurry to Bethlehem and see the son of Mary!

(All) *See his star shining bright*
  In the sky this Christmas Night!
  Follow me
  Joyfully;
Hurry to Bethlehem and see the son of Mary!

(Choir) 2 Angels bright, come from heaven's highest glory,
Bear the news with its message of good cheer:
'Sing, rejoice, for a King is come to save us,
  Hurry to Bethlehem and see the son of Mary!'

(All) *See his star shining bright,* (*etc.*)

(Choir) 3 See, he lies in his mother's tender keeping;
Jesus Christ in her loving arms asleep.
Shepherds poor, come to worship and adore him,
  Offer their humble gifts before the son of Mary.

(All) *See his star shining bright,* (*etc.*)

(Choir) 4 Let us all pay our homage at the manger,
Sing his praise on this joyful Christmas Night;
Christ is come, bringing promise of salvation;
  Hurry to Bethlehem and see the son of Mary!

(All) *See his star shining bright*
  In the sky this Christmas Night!
  Follow me
  Joyfully;
Hurry to Bethlehem and see the son of Mary,
Hurry to Bethlehem and see the son of Mary!

John Rutter (*b.* 1945)

39 Shepherds, in the field abiding

1. Shepherds, in the field abiding,
    Tell us, when the seraph bright
 Greeted you with wondrous tiding,
    What ye saw and heard that night.

    Gloria in excelsis Deo,
    Gloria in excelsis Deo!

2. We beheld (it is no fable)
    God incarnate, King of bliss,
 Swathed and cradled in a stable,
    And the angel-strain was this:

    Gloria in excelsis Deo, (etc.)

3. Quiristers on high were singing
    Jesus and his virgin-birth;
 Heav'nly bells the while a-ringing
    'Peace, goodwill to men on earth.'

    Gloria in excelsis Deo, (etc.)

4. Thanks, good herdmen; true your story;
    Have with you to Bethlehem:*
 Angels hymn the King of Glory;
    Carol we with you and them.

    Gloria in excelsis Deo, (etc.)

G. R. Woodward (1848–1934)

* Have with you = I am ready to go with you

40 Silent night

1. Silent night, holy night,
    All is calm, all is bright;
 Round yon virgin mother and child.
 Holy infant so tender and mild,
 Sleep in heavenly peace,
 Sleep in heavenly peace.

2. Silent night, holy night,
    Shepherds first saw the sight:
 Glories stream from heaven afar,
 Heav'nly hosts sing Alleluia:
 Christ the Saviour is born,
 Christ the Saviour is born!

3. Silent night, holy night,
    Son of God, love's pure light;
 Radiance beams from thy holy face,
 With the dawn of redeeming grace,
 Jesus, Lord, at thy birth,
 Jesus, Lord, at thy birth.

Josef Mohr (1792–1848)
tr. anon.

41 This joyful Eastertide

1. This joyful Eastertide,
    Away with sin and sorrow!
 My Love, the Crucified,
    Hath sprung to life this morrow.

    Had Christ, that once was slain,
    Ne'er burst his three-day prison,
    Our faith had been in vain:
    But now hath Christ arisen,
    Arisen, arisen, arisen.

2. My flesh in hope shall rest,
    And for a season slumber:
 Till trump from east to west
    Shall wake the dead in number.

    Had Christ, that once was slain, (etc.)

3. Death's flood hath lost his chill,
    Since Jesus crossed the river:
 Lover of souls, from ill
    My passing soul deliver.

    Had Christ, that once was slain, (etc.)

G. R. Woodward (1848–1934)

42 The first Nowell

1 The first Nowell the angel did say
Was to certain poor shepherds in fields as they lay;
In fields where they lay, keeping their sheep,
On a cold winter's night that was so deep:

Nowell, Nowell, Nowell, Nowell,
Born is the King of Israel!

2 They lookèd up and saw a star,
Shining in the east, beyond them far;
And to the earth it gave great light,
And so it continued both day and night:

Nowell, (etc.)

3 And by the light of that same star
Three wise men came from country far;
To seek for a king was their intent,
And to follow the star wherever it went:

Nowell, (etc.)

4 This star drew nigh to the north-west;
O'er Bethlehem it took its rest,
And there it did both stop and stay
Right over the place where Jesus lay:

Nowell, (etc.)

5 Then entered in those wise men three,
Full rev'rently upon their knee,
And offered there in his presence
Their gold and myrrh and frankincense:

Nowell, (etc.)

6 Then let us all with one accord
Sing praises to our heav'nly Lord,
That hath made heav'n and earth of naught,
And with his blood mankind hath bought:

Nowell, (etc.)

English traditional carol

43 The holly and the ivy

(All) 1 The holly and the ivy
When they are both full grown;
Of all the trees that are in the wood
The holly bears the crown.

O the rising of the sun
And the running of the deer,
The playing of the merry organ,
Sweet singing in the choir.

(Women) 2 The holly bears a blossom
As white as any flower;
And Mary bore sweet Jesus Christ
To be our sweet Saviour.

(All) *O the rising of the sun, (etc.)*

(Men) 3 The holly bears a berry
As red as any blood;
And Mary bore sweet Jesus Christ
To do poor sinners good.

(All) *O the rising of the sun, (etc.)*

(Women) 4 The holly bears a prickle
As sharp as any thorn;
And Mary bore sweet Jesus Christ
On Christmas Day in the morn.

(All) *O the rising of the sun, (etc.)*

(Men) 5 The holly bears a bark
As bitt'r as any gall;
And Mary bore sweet Jesus Christ
For to redeem us all.

(All) *O the rising of the sun, (etc.)*

English traditional carol

44 The twelve days of Christmas

On the first day of Christmas my true love sent to me
A partridge in a pear tree.

On the second day of Christmas my true love sent to me
Two turtle doves and a partridge in a pear tree.

On the third day of Christmas my true love sent to me
Three French hens, two turtle doves,
And a partridge in a pear tree.

On the fourth day of Christmas my true love sent to me
Four calling birds, three French hens, two turtle doves,
And a partridge in a pear tree.

On the fifth day of Christmas my true love sent to me
Five gold rings,
Four calling birds, three French hens, two turtle doves,
And a partridge in a pear tree.

Continue cumulatively:

Six geese a-laying

Seven swans a-swimming

Eight maids a-milking

Nine ladies dancing

Ten lords a-leaping

Eleven pipers piping

Twelve drummers drumming

English traditional carol

45 Unto us is born a Son

(All) 1   Unto us is born a Son,
    King of quires supernal:*
See on earth his life begun,
    Of lords the Lord eternal,
    Of lords the Lord eternal.

(All) 2   Christ, from heav'n descending low,
    Comes on earth a stranger;
Ox and ass their owner know,
    Becradled in the manger,
    Becradled in the manger.

(Men) 3   This did Herod sore affray†
    And grievously bewilder;
So he gave the word to slay,
    And slew the little childer,
    And slew the little childer.

(Women) 4   Of his love and mercy mild
    This the Christmas story;
And O that Mary's gentle Child
    Might lead us up to glory,
    Might lead us up to glory!

(All) 5   O and A, and A and O,
    Cum cantibus in choro,
Let our merry organ go,
    Benedicamus Domino,
    Benedicamus Domino.

* supernal=celestial   from *Piae Cantiones* (1582)
† affray=frighten   tr. G. R. Woodward (1848–1934)

46 *While shepherds watched their flocks*

1 While shepherds watched their flocks by night,
  All seated on the ground,
The angel of the Lord came down,
  And glory shone around.

2 'Fear not,' said he (for mighty dread
  Had seized their troubled mind);
'Glad tidings of great joy I bring
  To you and all mankind.

3 'To you in David's town this day
  Is born of David's line
A Saviour, who is Christ the Lord;
  And this shall be the sign:

4 'The heav'nly Babe you there shall find
  To human view displayed,
All meanly wrapped in swathing bands,
  And in a manger laid.'

5 Thus spake the seraph; and forthwith
  Appeared a shining throng
Of angels praising God, who thus
  Addressed their joyful song:

6 'All glory be to God on high,
  And to the earth be peace;
Goodwill henceforth from heav'n to men
  Begin and never cease.'

Nahum Tate (1652–1715)

47 *Kings of Orient*

(The three kings) 1 We three kings of Orient are;
  Bearing gifts we traverse afar
Field and fountain, moor and mountain,
  Following yonder star:

(All) *O star of wonder, star of night,*
  Star with royal beauty bright,
Westward leading, still proceeding,
  Guide us to thy perfect light.

(Melchior) 2 Born a king on Bethlehem plain,
  Gold I bring, to crown him again—
King for ever, ceasing never,
  Over us all to reign:

(All) *O star of wonder, star of night, (etc.)*

(Caspar) 3 Frankincense to offer have I;
  Incense owns a deity nigh:
Prayer and praising, all men raising,
  Worship him, God most high:

(All) *O star of wonder, star of night, (etc.)*

(Balthazar) 4 Myrrh is mine; its bitter perfume
  Breathes a life of gathering gloom;
Sorrowing, sighing, bleeding, dying,
  Sealed in the stone-cold tomb:

(All) *O star of wonder, star of night, (etc.)*

(All) 5 Glorious now, behold him arise,
  King, and God, and sacrifice!
Heav'n sings alleluya,
  Alleluya the earth replies:

(All) *O star of wonder, star of night, (etc.)*

John Henry Hopkins (1820–91)

Deity pronounced *Dee-ity*

48 *A merry Christmas*

1 We wish you a merry Christmas,
  We wish you a merry Christmas,
  We wish you a merry Christmas
  And a happy New Year.

> *Good tidings we bring*
> *To you and your kin;*
> *We wish you a merry Christmas*
> *And a happy New Year.*

2 Now bring us some figgy pudding,
  Now bring us some figgy pudding,
  Now bring us some figgy pudding,
  And bring some out here.

> *Good tidings we bring, (etc.)*

3 For we all like figgy pudding,
  For we all like figgy pudding,
  For we all like figgy pudding,
  So bring some out here.

> *Good tidings we bring, (etc.)*

4 And we won't go till we've got some,
  And we won't go till we've got some,
  And we won't go till we've got some,
  So bring some out here.

> *Good tidings we bring, (etc.)*

English traditional carol

49 *Ye choirs of new Jerusalem*

1 Ye choirs of new Jerusalem,
  Your sweetest notes employ,
  The Paschal victory to hymn
  In strains of holy joy.

2 How Judah's Lion burst his chains,
  And crushed the serpent's head;
  And brought with him, from death's domains,
  The long-imprisoned dead.

3 From hell's devouring jaws the prey
  Alone our Leader bore;
  His ransomed hosts pursue their way
  Where he hath gone before.

4 Triumphant in his glory now
  His sceptre ruleth all,
  Earth, heav'n, and hell before him bow,
  And at his footstool fall.

5 While joyful thus his praise we sing,
  His mercy we implore,
  Into his palace bright to bring
  And keep us evermore.

6 All glory to the Father be,
  All glory to the Son,
  All glory, Holy Ghost, to thee,
  While endless ages run.
    Alleluya! Amen.

St Fulbert of Chartres (*d.*1028)
tr. R. Campbell (1814–68)

50 *Ye choirs of new Jerusalem*

1 Ye choirs of new Jerusalem,
  Your sweetest notes employ,
  The Paschal victory to hymn
  In strains of holy joy.

2 For Judah's Lion bursts his chains,
  Crushing the serpent's head,
  And cries aloud through death's domains
  To wake th'imprison'd dead.

3 Devouring depths of hell their prey
  At his command restore;
  His ransomed hosts pursue their way
  Where Jesus goes before.

4 Triumphant in his glory now,
  To him all power is giv'n;
  To him in one communion bow
  All saints in earth and heaven.

5 While we, his soldiers, praise our King,
  His mercy we implore,
  Within his palace bright to bring
  And keep us evermore.

6 All glory to the Father be,
  All glory to the Son,
  All glory, Holy Ghost, to thee,
  While endless ages run.
    Alleluia! Amen.

OXFORD UNIVERSITY PRESS